Published by
24 ORE Cultura srl, Milan

Text by
Irene Cuzzaniti

Illustrations
Irene Rinaldi

Graphic design and layout
Rebecca Frascoli / PEPE *nymi*

Editing
Arianna Ghilardotti

English translation
Lauren Sunstein for Scriptum, Rome

© 2016 24 ORE Cultura srl, Milan

First edition April 2016
ISBN 978-88-6648-325-0

Printed in Italy

IRENE CUZZANITI

BUNCH UP!

A STEP-BY-STEP GUIDE
FOR BUDDING FLORISTS

illustrations by

IRENE RINALDI

24 ORE
CULTURA

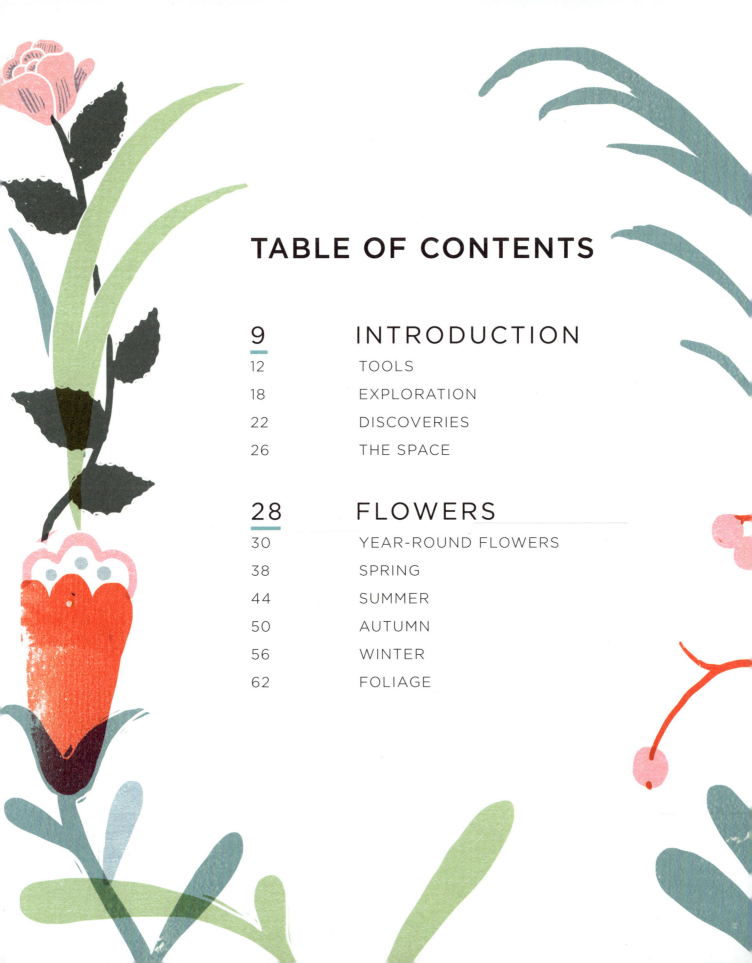

TABLE OF CONTENTS

70 DO IT YOURSELF

INTRODUCTION

Before being committed to paper and becoming the manual you are about to read, *Bunch up!* was a workshop held in Milan at the Spazio bk Bookshop and then again at my Fioreria alla Cascina Cuccagna.

When I first had the idea, I thought about how wonderful it would be to share the secrets of my trade, which I am convinced is good for the soul: making people feel more comfortable with flowers, teaching them how to identify them and to appreciate their differences, so they can choose wisely. What's more, I hoped to give my students the tools to observe nature with new eyes and to translate that new awareness into floral compositions. This book is inspired by those same hopes. We may or may not have an innate sense of beauty, of correct proportions and harmony, or a flair for combining colours, shapes and textures, but luckily, there are rules to help us.

One of those rules that should be followed as faithfully as possible is to work with products that are in season, which also means consuming responsibly. To this end, you need to consider the landscape and climate as well as all the signs coming from the plant world. You must open your eyes wide and extend your senses in all directions: first look at the trees, then the flowerbeds, the walls and sidewalks; pick up some branches, a stone, a feather, some berries. For our creations, we will use anything that has inspired an idea or touched us with an emotion. In each one, we will instil a feeling, the results of an exploration, an idea and a personality. And naturally, lots and lots of flowers.

The flowers that can be found in their natural habitat are of necessity limited by the season, wheras the market can offer a greater variety. This book, as a guide to buying seasonal flowers, features photographs of the individual flowers, season by season, which will make it easier to memorize their names. You will find history and myths about them as well. It should not be forgot, though, that while the flower may be a plant's "masterpiece", the pods, leaves, branches and even roots may make the perfect addition to your composition.

Once you have come up with some ideas and procured the flowers, it is time to compose. But how? You will quickly realize that the vase, the light and the space where you intend to place the flowers will all be there affecting you as you work. Fine! Continue to observe everything carefully and delicately at the same time. On the other hand, to make beautiful bouquets, you will also need to know the techniques that underlie every type of decoration, which require a bit of practice. All the secrets of the trade can be found here in this book, but as always, the important thing is to set yourself up with the right materials and not to overdo it or try to accentuate the features of every single element. Each one is unique and beautiful, even with its imperfections. You can try to straighten out a supple branch all you want, but it will always tend to return to its original position. Likewise with flower stems. So why not just go along with nature?

The shapes, colours, and hues of the flowers themselves can all serve as inspiration, but other seemingly unrelated sources of emotions, like a book or a melody, can also inspire and be translated into a bouquet. I have had the luck to be born in the heart of Rome, steeped in a crumbling, timeless beauty. It is often contradictory, though. Of course you have all the classic canons and proportions of the architecture, frescoes, decorations and piazzas of historic Rome, and yet, this is a city that never takes itself completely seriously and what Romans probably care about most is enjoying life.

Regardless, there is always something to discover in Rome, not least its fantastic amount of green spaces. To escape the bustle of the city, you can always take refuge in one of the many parks, each with its distinctive features: a crooked old tree, diseased but still standing strong, a thick woods where you can collect bits of bark and pine cones, marsh plants, poisonous plants, invasive plants, straggly flowers and flowers that are blooming in glory. It is here that my passion was born, so it is no wonder that landscape and gardens became my field of study in university and the focus of my professional life.

Today my love for it all continues just as instinctively and passionately as when I was young.

For me, the art of flowers encompasses so much: the spontaneous gesture and the well-planned production, technique and inspiration, rules and emotions.

"Each time it is as if we are about to enter a separate world buried deep inside us. That is the garden's gift," wrote the philosopher/gardener Jorn de Précy. Similarly, the ultimate ambition of this book is to help us learn something about ourselves while learning something about flowers.

IRENE CUZZANITI

TOOLS

What tools of the trade are necessary to allow complete creative freedom as you try your hand at the art of flowers?

SHEARS To cut tougher branches and, at first, flower stems as well, shears will be your best friend, a virtual extension of your hand. When you have gained greater dexterity, you can move on to a knife.

KNIFE If you prefer not to use your hands to eliminate thorns from roses and other flowers, you can use a well-sharpened knife. This will also prove useful for cutting branches at a 45° angle, thereby increasing the surface available for water absorption.

TWINE It is always best to use natural fibres to tie bunches of flowers.

SCISSORS Scissors are needed at the end to cut the twine after tying a bunch, but also to cut leaves and other soft vegetative parts.

FLORAL WIRE This absolutely essential item is used to hold up flowers with large corollas but weak stems, such as gerberas, or to thread together fruits, acorns and succulents in bouquets and decorations. Floral wire is available in a variety of lengths and diameters. Rolled wire is used for larger arrangements, such as festoons, wreaths, and runners.

SPONGE It is the most complete support for cut flowers, and useful for dried flowers as well. It is not a natural product, however, so it is best to use it sparingly. Cut it exactly to size, trying to keep waste to a minimum. Then leave it to soak in a clean container filled with water until it is entirely saturated.

KENZAN Traditionally used in the art of ikebana, this item multiplies your options for vases *ad infinitum* and allows you to achieve a dramatic effect with very few stems. You only need a few inches of water to ensure an elegant look.

CHICKEN WIRE This is useful as a base to be inserted in vases that would otherwise provide little stability to the flowers.

SINGLE-FLOWER PIPETTE As the name says, this is used to hold a single flower, but you can still create imaginative arrangements, for example, by tying the pipettes to branches. Beware: since they hold so little water, these pipettes dry out quickly!

FLORIST TAPE Very resistant and water-repellent, this tape is generally used to make a grid at the mouth of a bowl or wide container, creating a base for particularly flexible branches and difficult stems.

GUTTA-PERCHA This is a complicated name for an adhesive tape that expands almost magically, like crepe paper, thanks to the glue hidden in its folds. It is essential when preparing small bouquets, brooches and many accessories.

PINS For any type of decoration – be it a boutonniere, hair clip, pendant, bracelet or bouquet with satin-covered branches – pins are necessary to secure the tape exactly where you want it, eliminating the need for knots.

VASE The vase is your most important piece of equipment. To come up with a composition, you can start with a holder you already have in the house, which does not have to be an actual vase. A box, metal container, bowl, cup, or attractive bottle can also work well, provided that it offers a useful starting point from which to choose the flowers and the environment for the final composition. Regardless, the primary function of the vase is to highlight the flowers it holds.

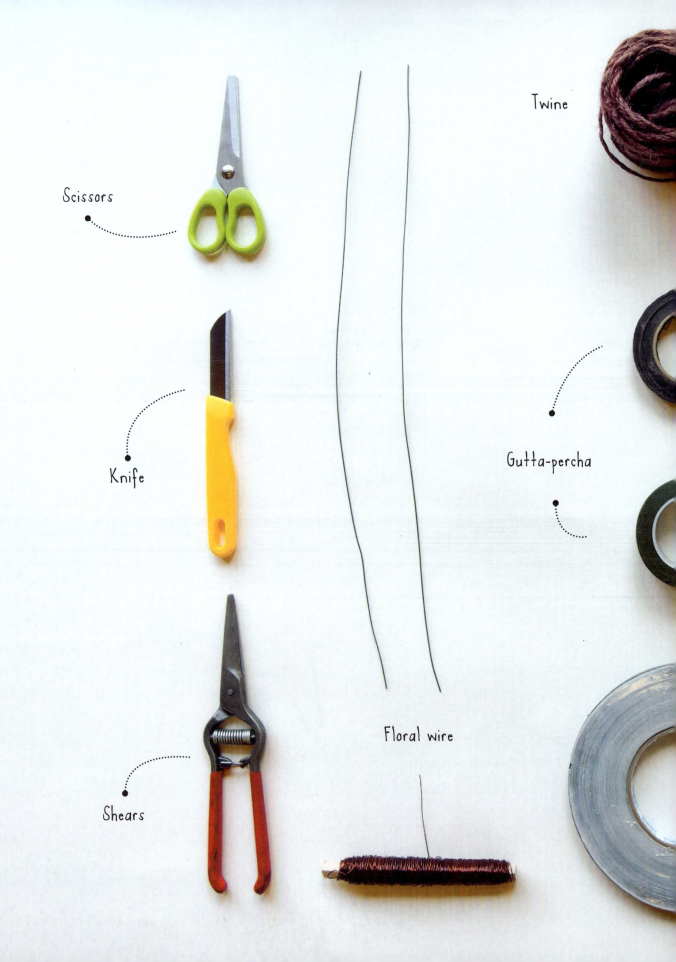

Scissors

Twine

Knife

Gutta-percha

Shears

Floral wire

Single-flower pipette

Pins

Sponge

Chicken wire

Florist tape

Kenzan

Jars and small bottles

Jars and small bottles are perfect solutions for informal contexts. Experiment with different heights and colours.

Unusual shapes

"Interpret" the shape and materials of your vase. Then position it to call attention to a place where no one tends to look otherwise.

Single-flower vases

A tall, narrow vase is the perfect receptacle to maximize the beauty of a single flower or flowering branch.

Bowls

Ideal for low tables or centrepieces. With bowls, you need to use chicken wire, sponge or florist tape to create a structure that can support the flowers. With particularly shallow bowls, it is best to use a kenzan.

Sets of small vases

You can use these sets for flowers that are all the same, playing with colour variations and different types of foliage. They can also be used for herbs, placing one type in each vase.

Round bowl

This is a classic, elegant solution, especially to position a very few flowers in architectural arrangements, such as lilies with their criss-crossed stems left visible, peonies arranged in a circle, or dahlias or tulips placed diagonally on top of each other. The effect is beautiful with floating corollas or a single lotus flower, but it is decorative even without flowers, filled for example with petals, rocks, or a striking leaf taken from an indoor plant.

Wide-mouthed containers

These containers are useful for airy arrangements, where all the elements are exposed. Place them in a large open space.

Pitchers

Although they are conceived for other uses, jugs, baskets and pitchers can look beautiful filled with greenery and flowers. If you are not sure that yours is watertight, cut a plastic bottle in half, fill it with water, and place it inside the larger container where it cannot be seen.

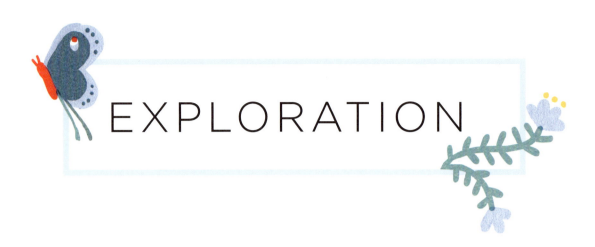

EXPLORATION

I walked in the woods
All by myself,
Searching for nothing:
That was my intent.
JOHANN WOLFGANG VON GOETHE

Inspiration for a composition or bouquet may come when you are choosing flowers at the florist's shop, or while you are on an excursion or a stroll, or even just doing errands in town. In fact, anything can become a source of inspiration: you just need to observe your surroundings with enough care and curiosity to see beyond the obvious. So, whether you are travelling or simply going from here to there, I invite you to be like explorers whose mission is to grab whatever catches their interest and capture it in some way – writing, drawing, photographing or collecting... The more willing you are to explore, the more abundant your loot will be. You will be surprised how easy it is to find interesting fragments, which means you can quickly gather a hoard of small treasures to serve as inspiration for new ideas.

Camera

Pen and pencil
with eraser

Notebook

Folding knife

Small jars
and vials

Compass

Envelopes and small
bags for collecting

Extra socks

Rubber bands
and ribbons for tying

Flask

DISCOVERIES

Make visible what, without you,
might perhaps never have been seen.
ROBERT BRESSON

In your comings and goings, you will quickly acquire a lot of material. What kind, though? And what should you do with it? Stones, feathers, pine cones, branches or pieces of bark, not to mention seeds, pods, and shells: basically what interests us are natural objects, since it is nature that we want to celebrate with our flowers.

You will figure out how to use the fragments you have collected simply by observing them from different angles and turning them over in your hands, or maybe dropping them or trying to break them. In fact, your exploration can continue long after you have collected everything. Any natural element can enhance a floral arrangement, giving it greater movement and interaction with its surroundings. Adding a few stones at the bottom of a vase recalls a stream; sand recalls the sea, while a bit of bark, an acorn or a layer of moss on the table evokes the essence of the forest. We can attach a feather to a branch with a bit of transparent wire, giving the illusion that it is about to fall, or we can place it in an abandoned bird's nest. Eggs and fruit can also be interesting, symbolic elements, though it is generally best to choose small ones.

Stones of varying shapes,
sizes and colours

Pebbles

Seeds

Feathers

Acorns

Porcupine's quill

Shells

Feather

Dried flowers

Wood

THE SPACE

Before you start assembling your composition, choose where to put it – in what spot in the house and then in what container. Remember, there are no right or wrong rooms for flowers. There are suitable arrangements for any environment, starting with wreaths to hang outside on the door, bunches of herbs for the kitchen, arrangements for the bedroom and even for the bathroom. In boutique hotels, floral decorations adorn every corner, from the landing on the stairs to the tables in the dining room. Why not treat ourselves to this pleasure in our own homes?

It is good to learn certain general rules about how to create balance and proportion, rules that inevitably are found in all the architecture, painting and photography manuals. Specifically, the subject should occupy one third of the space, which in turn should have an internal equilibrium; when altered, the overall appearance and meaning also change. Furthermore, keep in mind that the arrangement should be one or one and a half times as tall or wide as its container.

Sometimes, however, you already have an arrangement and you need to find the right spot for it. In that case, observe the shape, volume, colours and symmetry... Consider carefully how you want it to be framed or where in your home you would like to place an accent. Seek out a dialogue between the surface where you place the arrangement and the background that will serve to frame it, in effect, its portion of sky.

Always exploit the potential of empty spaces: do not simply dismiss them as empty. Think of them instead as open space, capable within limits of enhancing whatever it contains. It is in empty space that light expresses itself, modeling shapes and highlighting colours and materials. One's gaze can come to rest there, quieting the mind so that emotions can be felt more intensely.

Anyway, rules are made to be interpreted. So, first consider shape and proportion, but then indulge your whims; feel free to make mistakes. But most importantly, have fun!

FLOWERS

YEAR-ROUND FLOWERS

Now that you have looked around carefully and collected whatever strikes your curiosity or interest, and you have decided where to position your future arrangement, the time has come to think about flowers.

Just like fruit and vegetables, flowers are best when they are local and in season.

If we are drawing directly from Nature, of course, we have no choice, but at the florist's, we should try to buy only what is in season. That way, we help reduce the environmental impact of our purchases and can be assured that our flowers are fresh, and thus longer-lasting.

Still, you may sometimes need to buy a flower that is not in season, or want to add an exotic touch to your arrangement. The flowers found in shops year round are species that can be easily forced to bloom again, in response to market demand. Nonetheless, it is best to use them only when strictly necessary. Some of these flowers, like anthuriums and orchids, are quite striking and do better alone than in combination with other flowers. You just need to arrange them carefully in a holder that shows them off well, perhaps inserting a few green leaves and accessories around them. With only a few stems, you can create an impressive result.

The photographs on the following pages will help you identify the flowers typical of each season, flowers found year round, which should only be bought in special cases, and the principal types of foliage.

Lily

Anthurium

Freesia

Sunflower

St. John's wort

Baby's breath

Rose

Boat orchid

Gerbera

Peruvian lily

Gladiolus

Lisianthus

Carnation

"Green Trick" carnation

Dianthus Star Tessino

Sweet William

Dianthus raffine

Chrysanthemum
Bouncer

Chrysanthemum
Calimero pink

Chrysanthemum
Aurinko

Chrysanthemum
Jenny pink

Variegated
chrysanthemum

Chrysanthemum
Bautista orange

Chrysanthemum
Madiba

SPRING

Just as the day begins with the morning, the year begins with spring. In fact, in the ancient Roman and English ecclesiastic calendars, March is the first month of the year. This is when spring bulbs bloom, like tulips, daffodil, iris, the super-aromatic hyacinth, and the tall African lily with its magnificent lilac-blue. It is the time for ranunculus, columbines, and magnolias with all their flamboyant flowers. Lindens and acacia turn mottled with yellow blossoms and black locusts bend under their white blooms; the first daisies pop up, roses reveal their beauty, and the delphiniums attract all the bees. The first peonies are irresistible, and the anemones are gorgeous even when they start to fade.

You can play with the contrast between the cool colours of primroses, violets, and forget-me-nots and the warm, country colours of broom, forsythia, lilac and viburnum, or with the formal grace of calla lilies and freesia. You can use climbers to finish off your arrangements; a single branch of jasmine or Lady Banks rose has all the appeal of an entire plant, or even a long shoot of Virginia creeper or common ivy can do the trick. Inside, orchids burst into colour, while outside, on the patio or in the garden, hydrangea, rhododendron and azaleas put forth their glorious flower clusters. Meanwhile, besides trimming branches and stems, don't forget to plant new flowers! Choose a selection of perennials or easily-grown species that produce flowers that you can cut and enjoy as cut flowers: calendula, chamomile, pincushion flower, ornamental grasses and winter-blooming bulbs, such as crocuses.

Pansies

Plumbago

Chamomile

Rosa botanica

Daisies

Helipterum

Peruvian lily

Tulip

Anemone

Freesia

Peony

Daisy

Daffodil

Veronica

Hyacinth

Clematis

Wallflower

Lilac

SUMMER

Summer is thick, like an over-ripe spring, but less mild and more decisive.
These are the months when you are most likely to stroll or hike, when
opportunities to be inspired by nature abound. According to a tradition in magic,
the night of 24 June is the most favourable moment to gather herbs such
as St. John's wort, sagebrush, and holly, as well as dew.
If you follow the insects buzzing around the achillea, marigolds and zinnias,
you will be struck by the intensity of their colours and their particular shapes.
In fact, it is best to combine them sparingly.
The fields are carpeted in yellow and blue: put warm tones together, inserting just
a touch of blue, or vice versa, create a striking contrast, like in a Van Gogh painting.
Trim the foxglove and gladiolas so that they will last longer.
Dahlias grow in cottage gardens where the air is sweet with the perfume of
roses, lavender, chamomile, and countless tiny rosemary flowers. Nigella grows
in the countryside and pincushion flowers on the coasts; these small, delicate
blossoms can tone down flowers with a showy corolla and also work well
in festoons, bracelets, wreaths and other decorations.
Everywhere glows with life and calm in this season of powerful contrasts.

Celosia

Allium

Russian sage

Lavender

Crabapples

Artichoke

Butterfly bush

Wild carrot

Stonecrop

Cornflower

Nigella

Aster

Hydrangea

Curcuma

Astilbe

Hibiscus

Rose

Dahlia

Kangaroo paw

Craspedia

Yarrow

Sneezeweed

Chamomile

Helichrysum

AUTUMN

Autumn may be the most melancholy season of the year, but it is still so sweet.
Little by little, nandina, oak and mountain ash leaves turn gold or red. This months-long
spectacle of leaves falling from the trees is one of nature's most beautiful yearly shows.
Autumn is also the season of maturity. As the leaves are turning, fruits and berries are
ripening, in greater number than flowers, in fact, which are fewer though more versatile.
It is the time for long-lasting anemones, whose beauty lasts until the final black pistil
falls. Next come the chrysanthemums, considered a symbol of good luck in Asia,
with their huge corolla and long petals.
Keep an eye out for the delicate crocuses and tall, bright cosmos with their subtle
fragrance, which can be combined with racemes of pieris, Peruvian pepper tree and
viburnum. You can also put pomegranates among the flowers, leave one half open on
the table, or drop some seeds into the flower water (but then make sure you change it
often!) Buy some branches of cotton and, for contrast, place them with the warm or dark
colours typical of this time of year, or with other brighter hues, like those of the silver
ragwort or white heather.
Before the first cold spells of winter, you need to bed out the plants that will then delight
you with flowers in profusion in the spring, or even with the first thaw when it is still cold.
Some likely choices are snapdragons, bluebells, foxglove, sweet william, daisies, forget-
me-nots, primroses and wallflowers. Similarly, planting dahlia, hyacinth, daffodil, tulip, iris,
muscari, anemone and fritillaria bulbs is a simple task that will more than repay you five
months later!

Snowberry

Leucadendron

Leucospermum
cordifolium

Globe amaranth

Heather

Viburnum tinus

Japanese
chrysanthemum

Crabapple

Wheat

Nasturtium

Chrysanthemum

Cyclamen

Wild carrot

Pomegranate

Protea neriifolia

Brunia

Cotoneaster

Brassica

Abelia

Wax flower

WINTER

Perhaps the most wonderful thing about winter is its delightful smell of cold water and firewood. The painter Andrew Wyeth loved the cold seasons "when you can feel the bone structure in the landscape – the loneliness of it – the dead feeling of winter". In fact, there is something solitary and silent about nature in winter, and yet that doesn't make it sad – just more minimal. Nature is resting, and probably, if we could follow her rhythm – which is ours as well, after all – and just take it easy, we would love this season as much as the others.

This is the time to enjoy the rewards of the spring planting: the hellebore will keep us company all through the winter, along with the cyclamens and rex begonia with its beautiful leaves. Meanwhile, berries appear on the wintergreen and pyracantha.

At this time, you can sow delicate plants, like limonium, seemingly reserved for brides these days. Despite its frail look, this heavenly plant is surprisingly resistant, just like lady's mantle. Now is also the time to spread seeds for cosmos, craspedia and zinnia.

At Christmas, you can find amaryllis, ilex, hellebore, and branches of conifers in season. Although it is always best to favour seasonal plants, let's not forget those perfect representatives of winter – anemones, even if in nature they only bloom from April through June. My advice is to combine what you find, as always, resorting to flowers borrowed from the warmer season when necessary.

Camellia japonica

Skimmia japonica

Jatropha

Asian bittersweet

Sasanqua camellia

Winterberry

Poinsettia

Witch-hazel

Crocus

Beautyberry

Protea

Nerine

FOLIAGE

"Green, how much I want you green," wrote García Lorca, and nature is surely green. Holding a cut flower against a neutral background, observe it in all its simple yet extraordinary beauty. Then try putting it with one or more leaves – the tall, slender leaves of the gladiolus, or more simply, those of the salal, a variety of gaultheria frequently used by florists for its long life and regular ramification. Otherwise, you can use mastic leaves, which are small but numerous with an alternate leaf pattern.

If you are feeling more daring, however, you can opt for eucalyptus or grevillea, which like pittosporum, has long needle-shaped leaves whose silver-grey lower side contrasts strongly with the green upper side. Its red veins and thin, elongated leaves make it look rather like a flame. The eucalyptus, on the other hand, is an entire world in and of itself: there are so many, each more beautiful and fragrant than the other. Nonetheless, they are not so easy to use because they do not have a compact form.

Greenery completes, highlights and contributes discretely, calling our attention to nature as a whole. Experiment with everything that trees can offer: they are nature's most majestic architecture. With just ten or twenty small branches arranged in the middle of the table, you treat your guests to the pleasure of dining in the company of a live green festoon. Let yourself be inspired by fragrances, too: resins of conifers, oils released by the leaves of herbs, and the intense perfumes of the Mediterranean scrub.

Foliage is not so affected by the seasons, so you can find it year round without much effort. And you can always turn to the plants you have in your home: ficus, palmette, pothos, calathea or the ubiquitous ivy will all serve wonderfully to frame your flowers.

Beech leaves

Eucalyptus
paucifolia

Aralia

Eucalyptus stuartiana

Red oak

Beech leaves

Bear grass

Grevillea

Eucalyptus globulus

Eucalyptus parvifolia

Nandina

Lace fern

Lavender

Magnolia

Olive

Sage

Mastic

Medlar

Shatavari

Pittosporum nanum

Laurel

Rosemary

DO IT
YOUR-
SELF

BOUQUETS, BUNCHES AND DECORATIONS

What's the difference between a bouquet and a tied bunch?

A bouquet is round and compact; its structure is the same seen from any angle. The flowers are all the same height and arranged according to a regular pattern. The tied bunch, on the other hand, has a freer arrangement, resulting in more spontaneous, informal compositions.

On the following pages, you will see, step by step, how to create a variety of bouquets and bunches. Practice making the combinations suggested here, but once you have gained confidence with the technique, let your own taste guide you in your choices. There is no limit to the types of bunches you will be able to create with your favourite flowers.

Finally, you will find two demonstrations of how to create a boutonniere – that is, a pin with flowers like those worn by witnesses at a wedding – and also a delicate crown of flowers. After having created the bunches of flowers with the techniques outlined below, you will find these items quite easy to make. You will be able to add a floral accessory to your outfit in no time.

SINGLE-FLOWER BOUQUET

SEASON:
Summer

MATERIALS:
- 10 vuvuzela rose stems with buds

PROCEDURE:

1. Using a florist knife or shears, clean all the flowers – in this case, roses – eliminating only those leaves that would otherwise be in the water, that is, those below where the flowers will be tied. Make the cuts diagonally without crushing the stem so as not to obstruct the vessels that transport water. Remove as few thorns as possible, which helps the rose stay fresh longer.

2. Take a second stem and put it on top of the first, crossing them so that the corolla of the second flower points to the left and its stem to the bottom right. Continuing in this way with all the flowers, you will end up with a spiral bunch. This technique allows you to modify the position of the flowers as you work, raising, lowering, adding or removing them easily. The final look will be compact and formal.

3. Continue this way, adding the other flowers little by little and turning the bunch slightly clockwise each time. The place where you grasp the flowers and where the stems cross, known as the binding point, determines how tall the bunch will be. For a smaller, compact bunch, grab the flowers higher up, or simply grab them lower down for a taller, more open bunch.

4. After you have added all the flowers, check that you have the shape you want. For a uniformly shaped bouquet, turn the bunch upside down and rest the corollas gently on your free hand to even them out.

5. Now, tie the bunch securely, wrapping a piece of twine around the binding point. The knot should be

made quickly and be as
small and tight as possible.
Remove any damaged leaves
and regulate the length of
the stems with the knife,
cutting them as diagonally
as possible. In a well-made
spiral, the stems will all
be oriented in the same
direction: once you have
evened out the cut,
the bunch should be able
to stand upright unaided,
if you want.

BOUQUET WITH FLOWERS AND FOLIAGE

SEASON:

Year-round

MATERIALS:

* 10 lisianthus stems
* 5 eucalyptus branches

PROCEDURE:

1. Clean the lisianthus flowers by cutting off the leaves. Take one stem and put it with one eucalyptus branch.

2. Turn your wrist slightly and add a second flower, trying to cross it over the first; then add a third, keeping the distance between flowers regular. Continue adding one flower for each cardinal point, making sure not to grasp them too tightly.

3. Look at the top of the bunch and add foilage or blossoms to the empty spaces, keeping in mind that the final result should be quite homogeneous and regular.

4. Now look at the bunch from the front. Regulate the height of the flowers and eliminate low leaves. If necessary, trim any greenery that blocks the flowers. Make your cuts where the leaf attaches to the stem or branch so that no naked branch is left visible. Regulate the cut, shortening all the stems to the same height. Remember to cut diagonally.

3

4

SINGLE-COLOUR BOUQUET

SEASON:

Spring/summer

MATERIALS:

- 4 branched roses
- 2 Peruvian lilies
- 1 stem of chamomile

PROCEDURE:

1. Clean and prepare the flowers. It is important that the cut always be made between nodes, which makes it easier for the plant to absorb water. Take three rose stems and cross one over the other to create an initial small bunch.

2. Turn the bunch and add one Peruvian lily stem, so that it stands a bit higher than the roses.

3. Turn your hand and add the other Peruvian lily stem opposite the first.

4. Check the top of the bunch and regulate the height and distribution of the flowers accordingly. If the bouquet is not yet perfectly round, add a stem of chamomile or other small, branched flower that does not call attention to itself too much, yet still gives your bouquet more rhythm.

MIXED-FLOWER BOUQUET

SEASON:

Spring/summer

MATERIALS:

- 3 stems of stonecrop
- 1 stem of branched chrysanthemums
- 2 dahlias
- 1 carnation
- 3 roses with small blossoms
- 1 small branch of grevillea
- 1 small branch of eucalyptus

PROCEDURE:

1. Criss-cross the stems of stonecrop to create a uniform base.

2. Look at the top of the bunch and add the chrysanthemums or other branched flowers.

3. Add the dahlias, a bit lower than the branched flowers, to create movement and depth. Then add a particularly compact carnation.

4. Distribute the three roses opposite the chrysanthemums to balance and enhance the composition. Finally, adorn throughout with a bit of tall greenery that stays upright. Choosing two very different greens will help enliven this monochromatic bouquet.

TALL BUNCH

SEASON:

Summer/autumn

MATERIALS:

- 4 Peruvian lilies
- 2 gentians
- 2 asters
- 2 mottled lisianthus

PROCEDURE:

1. Choose tall, slender flowers that allow you to play with three contrasting or complementary colours. Take one stem of aster and add one Peruvian lily slightly lower.

2. Turn the two stems 20°. Opposite the Peruvian lily, add a flower with complementary colours, such as gentian, placing it so that it is higher than the Peruvian lily but lower than the aster.

3. Turn the bunch again and add a flower that will work as a binding element between all the flowers used so far: a lisianthus, which picks up the hues of the aster and gentian and is branched like the Peruvian lily. Try to insert it precisely in the centre of the bunch, slightly higher than the aster.

4. Continue inserting the other flowers in the same order: the last aster, another Peruvian lily, a gentian opposite the other gentian, and a lisianthus to give height. This bunch will end up with a pyramid shape, slightly rounded at the centre.

ASYMMETRICAL BUNCH

SEASON:

Summer/autumn

MATERIALS:

- 2 hydrangeas
- 1 stem of wax flower
- 3 moderate-sized roses
- 3 blades of bear grass
- 1 branch of medlar

PROCEDURE:

1. Bring together the two hydrangea stems being careful not to crush the flowers.

2. Place the wax flower beside the two hydrangeas, slightly higher and fan-shaped, with its branches tilted and wide open. When necessary, gently open the branches wider from below.

3. Tilt the bunch slightly and add the roses beside the wax flower. Make sure they are quite tilted and at the same height as the hydrangeas.

4. As always, check the top of the bunch to see where it needs more filling and where to place the foliage. Placed behind the roses, three blades of bear grass will be enough to give movement and a touch of irony to the composition.

5. Finally, to frame the bunch and hold it together, place a medlar branch with large, outspread leaves. The dark leaves contrast nicely with the paler hues of the flowers.

FAN-SHAPED BUNCH

SEASON:

Summer/autumn

MATERIALS:

- 3 Peruvian lilies
- 2 asters
- 1 gladiolus

PROCEDURE:

1. Clean the stems of the flowers up to a bit beyond the halfway mark. Then cross one Peruvian lily stem over the aster in such a way that its top stands higher than the Peruvian lily.

2. Add the flowers, grasping them high up and continuing to alternate asters and Peruvian lilies.

3. Adjust the point where you are holding the bunch: looking at the top of the bunch, the stems should form an oval, not a circle.

4. Choose the "front" of the bunch and add the gladiolus in such a way that all its flowers can be seen.

LOOSE BUNCH

SEASON:

Autumn/winter

MATERIALS:

- 3 hellebore flowers
- 2 branches of viburnum tinus with berries
- 2 branches of viburnum tinus with blossoms
- 3 branches of eucalyptus

PROCEDURE:

1. Cross two similarly-branched hellebore stems. Place one on top of the other, holding them low down and separating them as far apart as possible.

2. Add the two branches of viburnum tinus with berries to the right and left (again, choosing two similar ones), placing them slightly lower than the hellebores but following their lines.

3. Add another hellebore to the front and the viburnum with blossoms where the viburnum with berries left empty spaces. Decorate freely with the eucalyptus.

Now turn the bunch and observe it: it should be regular with no empty spaces, but not static or dull. Leave a few flowers sticking up higher (perhaps a hellebore), making sure to balance it on the opposite side with a branch of foliage drooping downwards.

BOUTONNIERE

SEASON:

Autumn/winter

MATERIALS:

- 1 small branch of mimosa
- 1 small branch of pyracantha berries
- 2 small brunia blossoms
- 1 base for boutonniere pin
- (available in shops selling articles for florists)
- 1 pin
- Thin satin ribbon
- Gutta-percha

PROCEDURE:

1. Take the mimosa and place it on the pint to determine where you need to cut it. Arrange and cut in such a way that the pin is completely hidden by leaves.

2. Make a mini-bunch with the mimosa and tie it with the gutta-percha, which will also serve to secure the bunch to the pin base. Stretch the ribbon well to make it stick better, but don't grip the bunch too tightly.

3. Add a few berries or a small flower (alternatively, flower clusters of stonecrop or St. John's wort, a little wax flower or globe amaranth all work well). Cover all the visible stems and the green of the gutta-percha with the satin ribbon.

4. Use the pin to secure the ribbon. If it is too long, you can shorten it with pincers.

5. The classic criteria of composition are applicable even for small, regular decorations such as these. Proportions should be pleasing, and the shape and texture should complement each other. Meanwhile, the vivid colour of the berries gives rhythm and movement.

DELICATE FLOWER CROWN

SEASON:

Winter/spring

MATERIALS:

- 1 long stem of pink snowberry
- 4 stems of pale limonium
- 1 orange ranunculus
- Floral wire
- Thick wire to use as the base for the crown
- Pincers
- Gutta-percha
- Satin ribbon

PROCEDURE:

1. Measure the circumference of your head with the thick wire and cut it with the pincers. Next, make a small ring at each end through which to pass the ribbon for the closure. Remove the leaves from the snowberry branches and tie one to the base with the floral wire. Secure two more small groups of berries, keeping them equidistant.

2. Prepare several small bunches of limonium, holding them together with gutta-percha. Then secure them to the base with another piece of gutta-percha. You will not need floral wire for delicate, non-woody stems.

3. Now take a ranunculus, wrap floral wire around the stem, and very gently insert it under the corolla. If possible, pierce the stem as well and make it come out the other side. This way, it is less likely that the blossom will break.

4. Position the ranunculus on one side. Secure it with floral wire and cut any excess stem. Then cover the entire base of the crown with the bunches of limonium, placing them on top of each other in a way that hides the stems.

5. Finally, pass the ribbon through the rings at the base of the crown and tie it with a knot.

COMPOSITIONS

Inspiration for a composition can hit you anytime anywhere: you just have to be open to it. Let your gaze rest on everything around you, from big open vistas to small objects at your feet, from surfaces to the clouds in the sky. Observe plants and their parts up close; open or break them if you can, taking them apart to see their insides.

Art is another unending source of inspiration. Stand close to paintings to see how the paints were applied and to observe the lines of the drawing; then step back to take in the emotions stirred by the image as a whole. A comprehensive vision like this can help you understand the rules that hold for any type of composition. Consider the overall harmony, the equilibrium created by proportions and disproportions, symmetries and asymmetries. Observe how the colours are combined and the relationship between full and empty spaces; you will see that density or openness can change our perception completely. And of course, it is always helpful to observe the work of florists and to visit gardens created by experts.

IN THE MIDST
OF WINTER,
I FOUND
THERE WAS,
WITHIN ME,
AN INVINCIBLE
SUMMER

ALBERT CAMUS

AN INVINCIBLE SUMMER

As the summer comes to an end, the days become more changeable; the sky often seems uncertain, as it was when I made this composition. After a drizzly morning, the sun came out from behind the clouds and the quote from Camus came into my mind. I went out to the garden and gathered several stems of white cosmos and silver ragwort, thinking they would serve well to represent winter. Then, to have something that would stand high above this pale base, I cut a few stems of Russian sage and butterfly bush and a few pincushion flowers that I particularly love and use often. Then I just added some fennel and a few daisies to give a touch of yellow and placed the composition in a vase that looked like it was made out of cracks in the ice. The result was delicate and magnificent at the same time, and even smelled delicious!

Russian sage

Pincushion flower

Butterfly bush

Fennel

Stones

Wild carrot

Cosmos

Silver ragwort

AN INVINCIBLE SUMMER

SEASON:

Summer

MATERIALS:

- 6-8 branches of silver ragwort
- 3 stems of cosmos
- 2 stems of Russian sage
- 1 stem of butterfly bush
- 3 branches of wild carrot
- 4-5 branches of fennel
- 10 stems of pincushion flowers

to decorate:

- Stones
- Leaves and blossoms

PROCEDURE:

1. Cut the stems of silver ragwort so that the visible part is 3/4 the height of the vase and arrange them in the vase with the cosmos flowers. Keep turning the vase as you do, positioning flowers in every direction.

2. Place the Russian sage in the centre of the composition, cutting it so that it is the same height as the vase, or slightly taller.

3. Take advantage of the dark hue of the butterfly bush to create depth: use it to direct the gaze towards the top of the composition.

4. Now it's time for the yellows. Cut the branches of fennel the same height as the Russian sage. Then, complete the composition with the delicate pincushion flowers, which serve to accent the higher, airier part. Fill in any empty spaces with the wild carrot.

5. Don't forget to decorate the composition with some of your finds: in this case, stones paired with petals and corollas can symbolize the contrast between summer and winter evoked by Camus.

3

4

5

FLOWER SECRETS

PINCUSHION FLOWER

Everything about the pincushion flower is beautiful – all the varieties of its flowers, all its splendid colours – lilac, pink, white and deep purple – and even its fruit, a blackish achene, which is quite useful dried. Found in open countryside, arid fields, beaches, hills and foothills, this rustic plant truly needs very little to survive.

COSMOS

Although the cosmos plant itself is quite large, its leaves are minute and slender. Its petals release a delicate, pleasant smell of apples when rubbed. In phytotherapy, the extract is taken orally in the form of drops in an alcohol solution. Cosmos is also used in Californian floritherapy to help resolve language and communication problems, such as stuttering, and to improve the relationship between thought and speech in general.

WILD CARROT

After fecundation, the shoots turn red and close in on themselves in the shape of a bird's nest. In fact, the plant, which is considered like a weed, is sometimes called by the name "bird's nest". Historically, the purple found in the central part of the flower was used by miniature painters. In fact, the traditional varieties of the carrot had violet or greyish roots. It was not until the end of the 17th century, in Holland, that some farmers began to select seeds to give the vegetable its characteristic orange colouring in honour of William of Orange, who had led the country in its war of independence against Spain. Boasting a vivid colour and a sweeter, more delicate taste, the new variety of carrot quickly spread throughout Europe, replacing the earlier one.

BUTTERFLY BUSH

All those who love flowers, nature, and the insects that serve as a biological defense love the butterfly bush. Do you want to see butterflies in your garden? Plant a butterfly bush. You will also enjoy its abundant flowers and intense fragrance. Furthermore, it is said to have anti-bacterial, anti-allergenic and healing properties. If you cut a dried-up flower from the branch, it will divide in half and produce more flowers, as also happens with the cosmos.

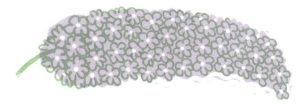

SUMMERS FLY, WINTERS WALK

CHARLIE BROWN

THE FLEETING SUMMER

Substantial and fiery, cockscomb never tires of lending its colours and vigour to the summer season. Even its etymology refers to the heat of summer as its official name "celosia" comes from the Greek *kelos*, or "burnt". This is probably an allusion to the flowers of the typical species of celosia, which look almost dried out.

In the language of flowers, the many varieties of cockscomb have the same symbolic value as the amaranth, that is, immortality and enduring emotions. When combined with roses, cockscomb represents the promise of eternal love, but even alone it conveys intensity, something intriguing and almost irresistible. In this composition, the cockscomb, piled on top of each other, look almost like they are trying to "escape", suggesting the dynamism of the hottest months of the year. Meanwhile, the robust stems and proud corollas recall their power – the other classic characteristic we associate with summer.

Sagebrush

Virginia creeper

Bluejay feather

Celosia

THE FLEETING SUMMER

SEASON:

Summer

MATERIALS:

- 10 stems of cockscomb of various colours
- 1 small branch of Virginia creeper
- 1 long sweet wormwood leaf

to decorate:

- 1 bluejay feather

PROCEDURE:

1. A metal vase would be ideal for this composition, but unfortunately, it is not recommended for use with flowers because the metal tends to blacken the stems. To get around this problem, place the flowers in a glass jar hidden inside a metal container.

2. Observe all the flowers before putting them in the water-filled jar. Line them up on the table and choose the best corolla with the healthiest leaves, which will become the focal point. Insert the first three flowers in the jar after cutting them at different lengths.

3. Insert the other flowers in order of height, cleaning off a bit of the stems if necessary to fit them into the jar, and alternating darks and lights.

4. Fill any empty spaces with the flowers that provide the greatest contrast in colour, in this case, yellow. This way you create a point of visual interest. Finish off with two touches of green and a feather from your collection to lighten up the composition and make it more dynamic.

TRICKS OF THE TRADE

EXPOSURE

Cut flowers should never be exposed to drafts or sun and other heat sources, which speed up water evaporation. Also be careful of the level of humidity in the room; either extreme – too dry or too humid – will make your flowers wilt. Since they prefer cool temperatures at night, it is good to put cut flowers outside the window in a protected place where the cool night air will revitalize them.

HEIGHT OF THE WATER

The level of the water for flowers with weak stems should be quite low. This holds for all bulbs and rhizomes, and in general, all stems that seem likely to get soggy in the water.

HOW TO DRY FLOWERS

There are only a few rules for drying flowers, but they are essential and should be followed carefully. First of all, flowers should be cleaned of leaves and thorns and then tied in bunches. Their number one enemy is humidity, so forget the basement or garage and put them in the attic or a very dry room with good air circulation instead. Enemy number two is light, so keep your flowers in the dark to ensure that their colours do not fade.

Drying times vary depending on the type of flower and on their environment, but you can assume that the bunches will be ready after one month.

I invite you to experiment. There are so many flowers and herbs that give surprising results!

Among the flowers that keep their original colours when dried are yarrow, amaranth, allium, globe thistle, eryngo, sunflower, helipterum, honesty, limonium, physalis, pampas grass, baby's breath, hydrangea, bulrush, protea, stonecrop, delphinium, lavender and herbs.

AUTUMN IS THE
MELLOWER
SEASON, AND
WHAT WE LOSE
IN FLOWERS
WE MORE
THAN GAIN
IN FRUITS

SAMUEL BUTLER

THE SWEETNESS
OF AUTUMN

The colours of autumn fruits perfectly embody this season of soft, golden light, when the leaves on the trees also put on a show of glorious warm colours. This is the season to tend to the earth's precious yields – time to harvest olives and grapes, to make fruit and vegetables left over from the summer into preserves and marmalade, and to enjoy the season's produce. Flowering plants, too, now provide us with berries and acorns. As they prepare for their winter repose, this is a precious chance for us to reflect on the life cycle of plants and their yearly transformation. This composition full of berries and fruits, conceived for a dinner party or simply to decorate your daily table, is a homage to the sweetness of autumn.

Chestnut

Pumpkin

Plum

Hazelnut

Dry sponge

Cornelian cherry

Brunia

Acorns

Oak gall

Pear

Persimmon

Chocolate cosmos

Marigold

Brassica or
Ornamental cabbage

Hawthorn

THE SWEETNESS OF AUTUMN

SEASON:

Autumn

MATERIALS:

- 1 long stem of dog rose
- 2 ornamental cabbages
- 3 small branches of Cornelian cherry or other bush with dark brown leaves
- 2 small branches of branched brunia with small blossoms
- 2 stems of brunia with large blossoms
- 5 small branches of dog rose with large hips
- 1 small branch of Lavalle hawthorn
- 2 oak branches with acorns
- 1 small branch with mast
- 2 marigolds
- 5 chocolate cosmos

PROCEDURE:

1. Cut the dry sponge to fit your container. Choose the most interesting dog-rose branch and position it to best effect, following its lines and emphasizing them. Place something at the base that balances the thrust of the dog rose.

2. Work on the base to make it more even and full, but not monotonous. Begin with the brunia; cut some stems taller than the others and insert them in small groups. Use the branches with brunia leaves as well. Fill the empty spaces with the branches of cornelian cherry or other bush with red or brown leaves, such as nandina or smoketree, or a few ivy leaves.

3. Now it's time to add colour and to play with the different heights to lighten up the composition and make it more surprising. Always remember to work from all directions. Before cutting the stems, measure them against the composition to determine what height you want to obtain, keeping in mind that one part will be embedded in the sponge. Use the less vivid colours, in this case the acorns and mast, to give greater depth.

4. Finish off your composition with seasonal fruits threaded on wooden skewers. Determine the quantity of fruit on the basis of the size of your container and the density of your composition. To give volume and

1

2

airiness, add a few small seasonal
flowers with delicate stems, which
make a pleasant effect when left
visible. In this case, I chose marigolds
for their very autumn-like orange
and very dark cosmos flowers to
create depth. You can enhance
your composition further with some
seasonal vegetables.

3

4

FLOWER SECRETS

CORNELIAN CHERRY

The edible fruits of the cornelian cherry are drupes with a single stone, like an elongated cherry but not as dark. Reaching maturity around October, they are good eaten immediately after picking or used to make jam. The wood of the cornelian cherry is the hardest wood in Europe and is used to make pipes, among other things. In Latin, the word *cornus* also means lance and javelin, both of whose shafts were often made with this wood.

DOG ROSE HIPS

This fruit of the dog rose (from the Greek *cynos*, dog + *rhodon*, rose) is actually a false fruit. At a certain point, the floral part turns fleshy and folds up, enclosing within it the actual fruits, which take the form of hairy achenes (the "seeds"). The shape, size and colours of the hips vary from one species to another and change as they ripen as well. Hips stay on the plant for a long time, although they are much sought after by birds, especially after the first winter frosts.

BRUNIA

The genus brunia comprises seven species native to South Africa. At first glance, it looks more like a berry than a flower, but its blossomed tips are as decorative as a corolla, not to mention that it produces attractive foliage in the vegetative stage. If you look closely at the base of the flowers, you might see a drop of the gummy nectar that bees, ants and other insects love so much. The plant holds onto its seeds all year until it dies, at which point they drop off. Brunia is a very ancient genus; in fact, some fossil traces have been discovered dating back to the era of the dinosaurs.

BRASSICA

This edible cabbage is surprisingly ornamental. Eliminating the leaves as they turn yellow, it is a perfect plant for autumnal bowls and boxes, mixed with cyclamens, heather, small chyrsanthemums, etc.

MARIGOLDS

Although they are indigenous to Mexico, marigolds are also known as Indian carnations, and indeed they are used extensively in Indian religious and civil ceremonies. The unusually pungent smell of the leaves makes them useful to drive nematodes out of infested soils.

TRICKS OF THE TRADE

FRUITS

Placing fruit near flowers speeds up the aging process because the fruits emit ethylene, a potent poison for flowers that causes them to wither. This explains why the only flowers used in the compositions you have just seen (conceived for a special lunch or dinner) were cosmos and the highly resistant marigold. Regardless, the flowers need to be replaced or removed as soon as they start to wilt, which will happen much sooner than usual, since they are set in a dry sponge, and thus without water.

DRY SPONGE

Sponges used for dried, stabilized, or dehydrated flowers are dry, hard, water-repellent and very resistant. They first came on the market in the 60s, before which a variety of specially-made bases were used, consisting basically of a metal grid filled with steel wool. Like sponges for fresh flowers, dry sponges come in many shapes and qualities, from deluxe to economical. There is also an environmentally-friendly version, which is hard to find but has the advantage of not crumbling. More rigid stalks can be inserted directly into the synthetic sponge whereas fragile ones need to be reinforced with a metal support. This is true for leaves, bunches of flowers, fruits, vegetables and all your finds. Also use metal supports to finish off a crowded composition: stems mounted on floral wire can be fit more easily into narrow spaces, so don't try to force them because they could easily break.

CONTAINERS

I used a handmade wooden bowl, which fittingly echoes the brown hues of the season. Furthermore, it is intentionally asymmetrical and the plants and other elements in it are also arranged with a great degree of freedom, creating a pleasing correspondence between the container and its contents.

TRUE HAPPINESS
IS TO ENJOY
THE PRESENT,
WITHOUT
ANXIOUS
DEPENDENCE
UPON THE FUTURE

SENECA

NATURE HERE AND NOW

In his wisdom, Seneca advises us to love what we have, when we have it.

The long-lived, noble art of ikebana is based on observation of and respect for nature, whose rhythm and harmony it reproduces in stylized forms. The concept of *hic et nunc*, here and now, has existed in every culture since ancient times; ikebana is a practice that expresses this specifically with plants. In this composition, the perfume of the roses and the powerful presence and soft colours of the dahlias, set against the Mediterranean shrubs, invite us to live the present moment to the fullest, without reservations or regrets.

Petals

Geranium

Wisteria

Oleacea

Rose

Acacia baileyana

Kenzan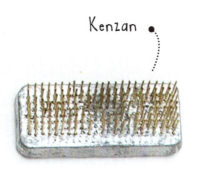

Small jar

Dahlia

Branched rose

NATURE HERE AND NOW

SEASON:

Summer

MATERIALS:

- 1 large, fragrant rose cream dream
- 1 white dahlia
- 1 stem of branched roses with semi-double blossoms
- 1 small branch of acacia baileyana
- 1 small branch of mimosa
- 1 small branch of wisteria
- 1 stem of muhlenbergia
- 2 small branches with very small leaves (I used an oleaceae)
- 1 geranium leaf
- kenzan

to decorate:

- Loose petals

PROCEDURE:

1. Make two small groups of greenery. The short-lived wisteria leaves need to be replaced often, so place them sideways, separate from the other stems, in a jar with water hidden inside the main container. On the other side, place the other branches of small-leaved foliage, securing them in the kenzan.

2. Secure the stem of branched roses in the kenzan, in the center of your container. Choose a stem with wide-open, slightly fading flowers as well as some unopened ones; this combination beautifully symbolizes the present moment, the inspiration for this composition. According to the precepts of ikebana, the bare stem of the rose should be left visible.

3. Work on one side. Place the rose cream dream so it leans out beyond the rim of the container. It should be almost closed, thus representing a magnificent present full of promise. Place the dahlia in the empty space between the roses, at an intermediate height. Its white fills the space well without weighing it down.

4. Add the last three small branches, leaning outwards. Finally, opposite the rose cream dream, insert the stem of muhlenbergia, as ethereal as a

fleeting instant. Under the dahlia, a few petals that fell as you worked can also symbolize the impermanence of the present. Add a stone to complete the composition.

TRICKS OF THE TRADE

KENZANS

Ikebana recreates in a vase the harmony of flowers growing in nature. This mission calls for precise rules of composition as well as special equipment, most importantly, a kenzan, whose name means literally "sword mountain". This accessory makes it possible to keep even the most rigid branches in the desired position, ensuring their stability. As it is made of lead or steel, the base stays clean and can be reused indefinitely. Originally, in order to hold the plants in place, a vase was filled with a bundle of straw. The kenzan gives a contemporary twist to the Japanese saying that the new adds to the old without replacing it: the stalks of straw are simply replaced with iron needles.

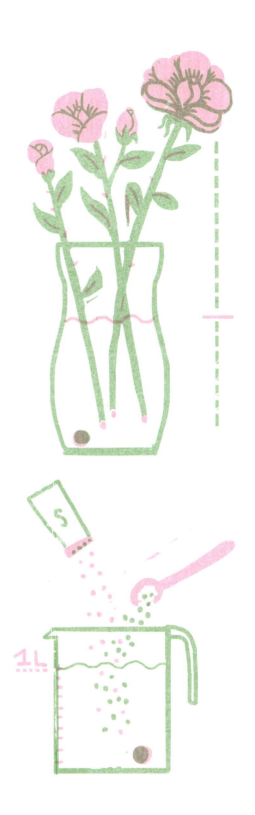

HOW TO KEEP ROSES BEAUTIFUL

To make your cut roses last longer, clean the stems of leaves and thorns thoroughly and cut them – never with anything but a knife – on a 45 degree angle, while they are immersed in water. Repeat this operation every two or three days, eliminating about 1 centimetre each time. Delicately remove any petals that have withered or blotched to keep the rot from spreading to the others.

Fill the vase with water – not too cold, though – up to at least 40% of the height of the flower and put a copper coin in the bottom. This will reduce the risk of fungal diseases to which roses are particularly vulnerable.

Personally, I encourage you to avoid any type of chemical product, including flower preservatives, bleach or chlorine, which are harmful to both the flowers and the environment. In their place, use a bit of sugar and salt (a teaspoon of each for every liter of water). Your roses will show their gratitude by keeping their beautiful vivid colours.

Another common household item, aspirin, slows down the transpiration of water inside the plant, which therefore stays more hydrated and lasts longer. Use a half pill for each liter of water. When a rose begins to fade, cut two centimeters off its stem. Then boil some water and immerse the entire length of the stem. When the water cools, put the roses back in the vase.

OF DIFFERENT COLOURS,
EQUALLY PERFECT,
THAT WILL APPEAR MOST
EXCELLENT,
WHICH IS SEEN NEAR
ITS DIRECT CONTRARY.
[...] BLUE NEAR A YELLOW;
GREEN NEAR RED;
BECAUSE EACH COLOUR
IS MORE DISTINCTLY SEEN, WHEN
OPPOSED TO ITS
CONTRARY, THAN TO ANY
OTHER SIMILAR TO IT

TREATISE ON PAINTING LEONARDO DA VINCI

ANEMONES AND CONTRASTS

When I read this quote, occasionally cited in manuals on colour theory, I immediately thought of anemones and the harmonious juxtaposition of their pale petals and dark pistils. Combining dark and light hues gives depth, while combining warm colours (which seem to move towards the viewer) and cold ones (which, vice versa, seem to move away) creates dynamism. The clear-cut primary colours create well-defined silhouettes, generating a visual play of geometries and asymmetries, balance and interaction. This composition is traversed by many lines, which are highlighted by the intense colour scheme. The only play of light is that coming directly from the colours and textures of the materials used.

Dog rose hips

Anemones

Dog rose

Wax flower

Viburnum

Pittosporum

Rosemary

Holly

Lace fern

Eryngo

Galax

ANEMONES AND CONTRASTS

SEASON:

Winter

MATERIALS:

- 6 stems of anemone, with mixed colours
- 1 stem of dog rose
- 1 stem of wax flower
- 1 stem of eryngo
- 2 small branches of pittosporum
- 2 leaves of galax
- 1 small branch di lace fern
- 1 small branch of holly
- 1 small branch di rosemary

to decorate:

- 1 small branch of viburnus tinus

PROCEDURE :

1. Choose a subtle vase that can relate to the colours of the flowers without overpowering them. Put the rosemary branch in diagonally to give rhythm and movement. Intensify the line with a small curved branch of holly, cutting it so that it is 3/4 as long as the rosemary.

Then add a whole eryngo stem even lower down to establish a focal point for the composition.

2. Now choose the largest, most beautiful anemone and position it in the centre of the vase, snugly fit among the eryngo and the foliage. Continue putting together the colours of the other flowers. You can cross them diagonally to give more movement to the composition, or group them, or both. Lay out the flowers on your work surface and regulate their height before putting them in the vase.

3. Use the foliage to give balance and stability to your composition. In the centre, insert two small, straight branches of pittosporum and one of lace fern with completely different lines, colour, and texture. A galax leaf placed behind the lace fern will serve to add depth.

To fill any empty spaces between the flowers in a vibrant way, insert the dog rose hips and the wax flower stem, leaving it rather tall and isolated; with its delicate look, the wax flower bestows a sense of lightness wherever it is placed. Finally, add some elements you have found: dog rose hips gathered as they fell or a small branch of viburnum tinum, the perfect resting place for a red anemone.

FLOWER SECRETS

ANEMONE

Anemone was a nymph in the court of Chloris, the goddess of flowers, who captured the heart of Zephyrus, the west wind of spring, and of Boreas, the north wind. In her jealousy, Chloris transformed Anemone into a flower doomed to open prematurely with strong gusts of wind. This explains why its name comes from the Greek *anemos*, or "wind".

This Greek myth was inspired by the transience of the petals of the anemone; this gorgeous flower has a notoriously short life, and in fact, it symbolizes short-lived emotions, the feeling of abandonment, anguish and betrayed love, but also of hope and expectation. Some species, in particular the wood anemone, are used in herbal medicine and homeopathy for cystitis, ear infections, insomnia, and gastric disturbances.

DOG ROSE

The dog rose is a wild rose that grows spontaneously in the woods. The flowers are lovely and the blossoms quite fragrant, but the stems, with their sharp, little thorns, are a bit alarming. This makes for a living oxymoron, reflected in its two distinct meanings in the language of flowers: on the one hand, grace and pleasure, on the other, pain and suffering.

Legend has it that the Roman god of wine Bacchus fell in love with a nymph and tried to possess her, as he was wont to do. She ran away in fear until she tripped on a shrub that held onto her as if to keep her from leaving. Since this allowed the god to reach his beloved, he expressed his gratitude by transforming the lowly shrub into a rose with flowers as delicate as the nymph's cheeks.

This plant is one of the Bach flowers, used to fight apathy. It is also used often in natural medicine for its calming properties.

ERYNGO

This genus of cardoons has mountain and maritime varieties, both of which have evolved mechanisms to defend themselves against herbivores. In fact, the Greek word *erungion* means "sea urchin", alluding to its thorny leaves.

Until the end of the 18th century, the candied roots of this plant, called eringos, were a popular delicacy in England. They were also believed to be an aphrodisiac, cited in this regard by Falstaff in Shakespeare's *Merry Wives of Windsor*. In the Renaissance, the eryngo represented eternal faithfulness, perhaps because it keeps its colour for so long when dried. In a self-portrait painted for his future wife, the great German painter and engraver Albrecht Dürer painted himself holding an eryngo.

COLOURS
ARE THE TRUE
INHABITANTS
OF SPACE

YVES KLEIN

A SENSE OF COLOUR

The theme of colour is crucial for anyone involved in the visual arts. Every florist, even a
impromptu or momentary one, ends up reflecting on this subject; indeed, our choice of colours
and their combinations reveals our taste more than any other choice we make.

Painters use their hands to mix colours and give life to the forms in their heads, while we must
draw on what already exists in nature. Nonetheless, it is a mistake to believe that, when working
with plants, our freedom to create forms and lines is limited: this is simply not true. There are
techniques and tricks to secure a branch in an entirely implausible position, to make it curve if it
is straight, or vice versa. We can certainly play with lines like patient sculptors, but this time let's
try starting with colour and making it the defining feature of our composition.

White lilac

Lilac

Guelder-rose

A SENSE OF COLOUR

SEASON:

Spring

MATERIALS:

- 5 stems of white lilac
- 5 stems di violet lilac
- 5 stems of Guelder-rose

to decorate:

- household objects

PROCEDURE:

1. Choosing flowers with loose, supple lines allows you to get better results from the planes of colour and to achieve an airy effect, rather than a compact one. For the base, we chose Guelder-rose, an umbrella-shaped flower that works particularly well arranged in cascades.

2. Decide on the sequence of blossom colours you want, keeping in mind that using the palest shades in the upper part of the composition helps soften the overall look. Distribute the violet lilacs on a horizontal plane opposite the Guelder-rose.

3. Add 3 stems of white lilac above the violet ones. To make it easier, cut the stems on the angle they will have in the container, in this case, 45° to the left. Create a spiral in the water so that the stems are stable. If necessary, gently help the flowers lean on each other, intertwining leaves, stems and blossoms.

4. Opposite the palest stems, add the last white flowers, slightly in back. Arranging groups of flowers into homogeneous masses of colour leads to a balanced and particularly harmonious composition.

4

TRICKS OF THE TRADE

INTERPRET THE SPACE

To make a composition like this that drops down on one side and rises up on the other, you need a container whose mouth is not too wide, but wider than the base. A wine glass fits this bill perfectly, as well as serving to lighten the composition and make it soar. The main line of the composition, being a diagonal, contributes a powerful sense of dynamism, but the end result can still be stable and balanced if you arrange the flowers symmetrically around this line. Don't forget to leave some empty spaces to soften and lighten the overall effect.

WOODY STEMS

With these types of long-lasting but delicate flowers, it is best to add some preservative to the water – though nothing chemical, of course! One teaspoon of lemon juice per liter of water will do the trick. To keep the water clear and free of bacteria, you can also use carbon or aluminium. You can also treat your blossoms to some precious nutrients by adding a teaspoon of sugar and a pinch of salt. On the other hand, if you want to delay the opening of the buds, keep them in a cool, not frigid, dark place. A refrigerator works well, but wrap the flowers in paper or a paper bag first. Finally, two cuts a few centimeters long should be etched crosswise into the woody stems every 2 or 3 days.

FLOWER SECRETS

LILAC OR SYRINGA

An ancient legend recounts that fairies used to plant a lilac to purify places where they thought evil lurked. While today lilacs, also known as syringas, are used primarily for decoration, they were used widely in the past for therapeutic purposes: the tea obtained from its bark lowers fever; an infusion made with its leaves relieves congestion, beneficial to both the stomach and the liver, while the oil obtained by macerating the flowers helps relieve rheumatic problems and minor pains. In addition, aromatic essences and perfumes are obtained from the flowers.

GUELDER-ROSE

The lines, resistence and variety of this species of viburnum are extraordinary. Found all the way from Europe to Japan, its berries constitute a major food source for birds.

These shrubs have something for every season: in autumn, their leaves turn a lovely reddish-yellow and in the summer, their gorgeous flowers – strongly scented hermaphrodites, not unlike hydrangea blossoms – grow into large, spherical blooms about 5-10 centimeters wide, usually white or green. After the flowering stage, plants with fertile flowers develop drupes, small, red fruits which, though toxic, are quite decorative and cling to the branches until winter. Nectar made by glands at the base of the leaves attracts ants, which actually serve to protect the plant from other destructive insects.

IT IS AN INTENSELY SIMPLE,
INTENSELY FLORAL, FLOWER.
ALL SILK AND FLAME:
A SCARLET CUP
[...] SEEN AMONG THE WILD
GRASS FAR AWAY, LIKE A
BURNING COAL
FALLEN FROM HEAVEN'S ALTARS.
YOU CANNOT HAVE A
MORE COMPLETE, A MORE STAINLESS,
TYPE OF FLOWER
ABSOLUTE; INSIDE AND OUTSIDE,
ALL FLOWER

FROM *PROSERPINA*, BY JOHN RUSKIN

AN INTENSELY FLORAL FLOWER

This is how the English writer, painter and poet John Ruskin defined the poppy, "an intensely simple flower", formed of four petals around a small pod that contains the black seeds used so often in cooking.

Classic symbol of spring and of delicate, ephemeral beauty, poppies stand tall in fields, bending in the wind, light yet strong, short-lived yet coveted. Their colours attract insects and men alike. It is hard to imagine how anyone can be indifferent to their charm. To highlight them, I chose a tall vase and looked for something that would complement them, a secondary flower, a kindred spirit, not a contrasting one. Here I chose clematis, a plant that is strong and even invasive when it is in a suitable environment though delicate when it is not. The two flowers harmonize perfectly: growing horizontally, the clematis makes a fine balance for the vertical line of the poppy.

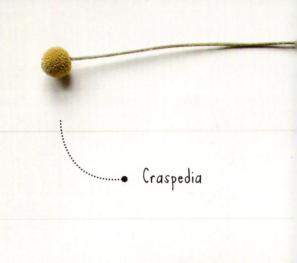

Craspedia

Poppy

White broom

Clematis

AN INTENSELY FLORAL FLOWER

SEASON:

Spring

MATERIALS:

- 10 poppies
- 5 stems of clematis
- 1 branch of white broom

to decorate:

- 1 craspedia

PROCEDURE:

1. Make a tall bunch of poppies, keeping in mind that the delicate buds will open gradually.

Choose the most open flowers as the focal point and develop the bunch so that it is slightly asymmetrical in order to leave space for the other flowers.

2. Use the clematis to extend the composition horizontally. Take one straight, branched stem with flowers at varying heights and insert it among the poppies on the right side of the bunch.

3. Arrange the remaining clematis to the right of the poppies. The inclination, and thus the line, should be the opposite of the other group of flowers. To get this effect, position them in a fan shape, leaning increasingly towards the horizontal and away from the other flowers.

4. Accentuate the movement of the composition and tone down the verticality of the poppies by inserting the stem of broom among the clematis. A craspedia resting at the foot of the vase gives a country feeling and calls more attention to the direction of the clematis.

TRICKS OF THE TRADE

POPPY STEMS

Field, or corn, poppies are wild flowers that are frequently sold at florists' but are also readily found in nature. In the latter case, they should be picked in the late evening, when the dew has evaporated, the air is fresh and the stems are swollen. If they are cut in full sun, the stems could have trouble absorbing water fast enough to keep from wilting. Even if they are cut in the morning after an abundant dew, they sometimes shrivel up anyway.

Once cut, immerge the poppy stems in water as soon as possible so that the ends do not have time to dry. Leave them for a minute in two fingers of boiling water; then fill the container with tepid water up to the rim and leave the flowers soaking for a few hours. This method works also for roses, marsh mallow, leaves of tropical plants, poinsettia, and other plants that secrete lymph.

FLOWER SECRETS

CLEMATIS

To have longer-lasting clematis, choose woody or semi-woody stems with flowers that have not yet opened all the way. Then eliminate most of the foliage to limit transpiration, and immerge the whole stem (including the flower) in a large bowl filled with cold water for about 10-12 hours before using it. Some varieties, including all the botanical species of clematis and the herbaceous perennials, are especially desirable for cutting since at the end of the season, the blossoms are replaced by attractive seed pods, whose spherical shape and silky feel make them an appealing element in dried flower arrangements.

POPPIES

People have always attributed symbolic qualities to poppies: white poppies represent consolation; red ones, oblivion or imagination; yellow ones, wealth and success, and pink ones, vivacity. According to tradition, they are also a symbol of sleep: in fact, the god Morpheus is sometimes represented carrying a large bunch of poppies.

In the United Kingdom, poppies are considered the flower of memory, especially the memory of soldiers who fell in war. On Remembrance Day, celebrated on the second Sunday of November, the custom is for people to wear a poppy in their buttonhole and place a crown of poppies on the war cenotaphs.

Although they are native to the Mediterranean and Middle East, poppies have been cultivated in western and northern Europe for many centuries. Opium poppies were already well-known in the 15th century for their narcotic properties and later, many species were cultivated in Victorian gardens, including the Iceland poppy (which is actually native to Siberia). The petals are used in cooking as decoration, and the leaves, which have a slightly nutty taste, are eaten raw in salads or cooked like spinach. For consumption, poppies should be gathered in early spring, when the plant is still young and flowerless. In addition, the syrup of the petals helps relieve coughing.

WE ARE
BUT JOKES
OF LIGHT

MEDARDO ROSSO

THE TOUCH OF LIGHT

When light gently touches down on a surface, it materializes and gives shape and solidity to whatever it touches. There is a constant, indissoluble bond between ourselves, the world we see, and light. In fact, thinking about light should never be considered trivial; on the contrary, it is too often taken for granted. So let's amuse ourselves with monochrome tones, focusing attention on the light, which will bring out all the qualities of our raw materials. In fact, in a composition of flowers, leaves and branches, light is just as decisive a factor as the shapes, volumes, geometries and textures of the materials themselves. The difference is that we cannot control the light – and therein lies its beauty.

Artichoke

Beetroot

Black carrot

Rex begonia

Amaryllis

Red chard

Radicchio di Treviso

Kale

THE TOUCH OF LIGHT

SEASON:

Winter

MATERIALS:

- 3 artichokes, at least one with leaves
- 1 radicchio di Treviso
- 3 black carrots with leaves
- 2 heads of kale
- 1 red chard
- 1 beetroot
- 1 red amaryllis
- 1 rex begonia leaf

to decorate:

- 1 red beetroot

PROCEDURE:

1. In this season, florists and nature offer few options, but we still want to decorate our tables.

So why not draw from a produce market to create an edible composition with no flowers at all?

The star vegetable is surely the artichoke, thanks to its size and texture, so begin with them.

Rest them on their sides, on top of one another. Keep the leaves on at least one of the artichokes, providing a rare sight on our tables.

Now add something completely different on the other side: radicchio di Treviso, whose curvy leaves are perfect to hook over the edge of the container – not to mention their magnificent colour. Behind the radicchio, place the carrot leaves, which, like artichoke leaves, are usually discarded.

2. To complete the base of the container, place in the front a few leaves of kale and beetroot, letting them fall to the outside. Thus we create a play of differing textures, sizes and colours, obtaining enjoyable contrasts by placing them all together in this way.

To balance the pointy artichokes, place a round beetroot on the opposite side.

3. Now it is time to use your flower. If you put it beside the artichokes, you will see that it looks out of place. Better to put it beside the beetroot for a more balanced look. You also want to highlight the all-important amaryllis by placing some greenery; in this case, stand the other head of kale behind the flower.

4. Fill the two small empty spaces to the left and right of the red flower with the black carrot, wedging its rigid stems between the others. On the opposite side, place the rex begonia leaf, which are so splendid in this season. This one simple leaf is sufficient to harmonize the artichokes with the flowers. The composition is now quite dense, so finish off with just one more beetroot, whose stupendous leaves deserve a place of honour.

FLOWER SECRETS

AMARYLLIS

The amaryllis, with its long stem and magnificent blossoms, is associated with elegance, pride and dazzling beauty, but also with bashfulness.

Not only does it make a stunning addition to your home at Christmas time and throughout the cold season, but it is even easy to grow; I highly recommend giving it a try. Besides, it is thrilling to watch how the plant develops out of its enormous bulb, from when the first leaves emerge to when the first flower shrivels up and others come thereafter. Place your plant in a partially shaded place where it will get several hours of direct sunlight, and water it thoroughly every 10-15 days. It should be fertilized once

a month with an organic fertilizer rich
in potassium and phosphorus, but stop
fertilizing in autumn to ensure that late
growth of new vegetation does not make
the plant more vulnerable to the cold.
Be careful not to break the stem, which is
not as robust as it looks. As it is large and
hollow, cut it when it is immersed in water to
keep air bubbles from forming in the stalk.
Fill a bucket or large bowl with tepid water,
put the stem in, and, as always, cut it on an
angle with a small, sharp knife.

THE ORDER OF IDEAS MUST FOLLOW THE ORDER OF THINGS

GIAMBATTISTA VICO

THE ORDER OF THINGS

Vico invites us to begin with objective, concrete facts to reason or to find new ideas. Try observing very carefully something that you always see without really seeing. Sometimes we think we need to search who knows where for inspiration to create something new, somewhere outside of ourselves and the place where we are. On the contrary, it is more likely that the new ideas we seek will come from a conscious, thorough observation of our own work space or office. Look around: your desk is surely full of all kinds of little objects and their respective containers. Just think how you might use them differently. What effect would it have to see flowers in the little basket instead of those pens and pencils? We have seen how many unlikely containers can be used for our purposes; you only need to hide a jar of water inside. Let's follow the inspiration of the moment to create a cheerful, original composition.

Protea neriifolia

Leucospermum
cuneiforme

Stationery items

Brunia albifolia

Gnaphalium

Aulax cancellata

Berzelia
galpini

Berzelia
abrotanoides

THE ORDER OF THINGS

SEASON:

Autumn

MATERIALS:

- 1 protea neriifolia
- 2 leucospermum cuneiforme
- 1 gnaphalium
- 1 red berzelia galpini
- 1 aulax cancellata
- brunia albiflora leaves
- 1 berzelia abrotanoides

to decorate:

- stationery materials

PROCEDURE:

1. Observe your flowers and containers: they should be more or less on the same scale. Begin with the largest flower, the protea. In such a fragmented composition as this, it is essential that each small bunch harmonize perfectly with the others, that there be some sort of echo between the elements; otherwise the composition may just look messy. Thus what you put with the protea should be echoed in some way by the adjacent creations. In this case, use the white and yellow of the berzelia abrotanoides.

2. In the second little vase, put another large, attractive flower, the leucospermum, whose yellow picks up the yellow of the berzelia abrotanoides. Then add the gnaphalium to echo the pink of the protea.

3. Use the berzelia galpini, whose form recalls that of the brunia, as a base to put together a sort of tall bunch. Create height with the greenery of the aulax cancellata.

4. Use four different ingredients to create the last bunch for the smallest container. This one should be a synthesis of all the others.

5. Bring all of the vases to your desk, placing the largest in the back, the second largest in the centre and the two smallest ones on either side. What effect does it make now to see flowers in these objects you have been seeing every day? Subverting your daily routine for once inevitably offers a breath of fresh air, one that just may inspire other new ideas.

171

FLOWER SECRETS

NATIVE AUSTRALIAN FLOWERS

The flamboyant flowers in this variegated composition arrive on the market in pre-mixed bunches. Very reasonably priced, they make an excellent purchase to enjoy both as fresh cut flowers and to dry. These flowers have a long and fascinating history. In fact, they belong to the proteaceae, a prehistoric family, found only in the southern hemisphere, which originated some 300 million years ago. At that time, when dinosaurs roamed that part of the world, all the land masses were united in the vast southern continent of Gondwana. When the continents separated, so did the family of proteas. Thus today proteas are native plants in Australia, South Africa and Indonesia, but they have had plenty of time to evolve differently.

Some of the most commonly cultivated species are leucadendron, leucospermum, telopea, hardenbergia, ozothamnus, wax flower, boronia, and grevillea. Also on this list is the protea, the symbol of South Africa, a plant that grows well in flowerpots and in Mediterranean climates, protected from the wind, like citrus trees.

FLORAL ESSENCES

Australian aborigenes were familiar with a large variety of floral essences, in which they placed enormous faith. Generally, they would seek the benefits by eating the entire flower; if the species was not edible, however, they would absorb its therapeutic vibrations by sitting on it!

Using as many as 84 different essences, floratherapy with Australian flowers is particularly effective for treating pain. The power of these floral essences originates with the unpolluted environment of the Australian bush, home of the plants used for extraction. Unlike other vast territories of the planet, in fact, Australia has remained practically uncontaminated by nuclear waste and chemical pollution. Furthermore, many of its flowers are protected by law. Despite all this, however, it is believed that this millennial family of plants is slowly dying out. All the more reason for us to grow them!

ELEGANCE IS THE
BALANCE
BETWEEN
PROPORTION,
EMOTION,
AND SURPRISE

VALENTINO GARAVANI

THE ELEGANT SURPRISE

Elegance is synonomous with harmony and timelessness, but not necessarily with a classic look. Something unexpected may capture our attention, which we recognize as original or at least not obvious. I wanted to emphasize this particular characteristic, cited by the master of fashion Valentino Garavani, to introduce a composition that is quite different from those you have seen before. This one occupies a large space of the surface on which it is arranged – a mini-installation with references to the natural world all mixed together with references to the world of men. Autumn leaves clinging to their branches are always elegant, perhaps even more so than flowers, thanks to their simplicity and proportion.

Finally, don't forget the harmony of proportions as you work. Make the composition longer, shorter, wider or narrower, in correspondence to the surface being decorated, but do not exceed one third of the entire space.

Green pepper

Copper saucer

Tillandsia
stricta

Stabilized beech

Galax

Tillandsia
caput-medusae

Pine cone

Honesty

Spanish moss

Tillandsia bulbosa

Tillandsia xerographica

Tillandsia brachycaulos multilflora

Tillandsia Juncifolia

THE ELEGANT SURPRISE

SEASON:

Year-round

MATERIALS:

- 1 short and 2 long branches of stabilized beech
- 13 different types of tillandsias
- 7 leaves of galax
- 1 bunch of honesty
- 1 pine cone
- several small branches of Peruvian pepper tree

PROCEDURE:

1. The branches of stabilized beech will form the base of your composition. As they are always slightly curved and do not rest flat on the table, they are useful to add volume. Playing a bit with their spectrum of warm tones, create a meandering, airy base with the long branches, being careful not to make it too wide. Extend it along a slight diagonal, reinforcing the natural twists and turns of the branches to give greater depth to the overall arrangement. In the centre, lay the shorter branch, which will also serve to cover the naked stems of the other two branches.

2. When you are pleased with the base, continue with the tillandsia xerographica – the largest, showiest element – placing it at one end of the table. Then take all the remaining tillandsias, which though smaller should be just as dynamic, and place them so that they follow the shapes of the branches; slip them under the leaves or lay them on the surface, but try to avoid any vertical lines. The final result gives a rare sense of immediacy and impermanence.

3. Use the pine cone in the opposite corner from the xerographica in order to balance the mass well. The galax leaves with their soft, curious shape provide a cheerful accent, in contrast with the warm tones of the beech leaves.

4. Finish by placing a bunch of honesty in a tall container in a corner, a bit in the background. Being such a different colour and material than the rest, these flowers are perfect to add an element of surprise. Beside the tall thin vase, place a similarly slender one with small red pepper branches cascading over the edge; you will find that the two opposites balance each other out. Now all you have to do is sit down at the table and enjoy your composition.

4

FLOWER SECRETS

TILLANDSIAS

Originally from Central America, Tillandsias are epiphytes, that is, they grow without soil, attached to the trunk or branches of trees. In their native regions, they even grow on electric wires and television antennas. These airplants absorb humidity from the air through small filaments on their leaves called trichomes, which give the plant its velvety appearance.

In addition to humidity, tillandsias also capture fine dust in the air along with the polluting agents in it. Many studies have shown, however, that they are capable of absorbing, metabolizing, and eventually eliminating these particles. These plants require little care, although they do need to be misted often in the summer, preferably with rainwater left to decant for a few days. In winter, they only need misting about once every two weeks. Wet the base of the plant, not the centre.

Tillandsias are monocarpic plants, which means they only flower once in their lives, like wheat, corn or pineapple. After flowering, new shoots appear along the stem with traits identical to the mother plant.

PINE CONES

The fruit of the pine tree is loaded with symbolic meanings. The sturdy wood, the resin and the leaves that stay green all year round suggest an association with life force and immortality. In this regard, rural traditions consider it good luck to give a bunch of pine cones tied together to be hung over the door of a house to protect the family living there. The pine cones' oval shape and abundance of seeds also associate them with fertility. In the Near East, pine cones were used in purification rites, while in the Greek world, they were one of the attributes of Dionysus, the god associated with the mysteries of death and rebirth or regeneration.

HONESTY

A biennial plant despite its Latin name (Lunaria annua), honesty symbolizes fickle emotions and neglect. Like its English name, however, it also represents honesty, probably due to the transparency of its fruit, a flat, round seed pod whose black seeds show through clearly. As time passes, these fruits lose their colour and solidity, becoming increasingly silvery and ethereal.

Honesty are gathered in summer from the woods and wetlands where they grow. To dry, they should be placed upside down in a place that is not too dark. A mother tincture produced from the air parts of the plant is used in herbal medicine and phytotherapy to defend against scurvy and nausea, while the leaves and roots are eaten cooked or in salad for their diuretic properties. The strong-smelling seeds are also used to make a particular type of mustard.

TRICKS OF THE TRADE

STABILIZED FLOWERS

The patented stabilization process involves substituting the liquid inside the flower with compounds that block growth, and thus the natural process of decay, without altering the flower's texture or beauty. The procedure takes time since it must be performed gradually and with the correct mix of substances to achieve quality results. However, stabilized flowers are a fully natural product, which means that all the imperfections found in nature before the process will still be there afterwards. If kept in the appropriate conditions, stabilized flowers keep their beauty intact for up to four years.

THE PROCEDURE

Wash the flowers with water to eliminate dust and dirt.

Cut 2 centimetres from the stem to eliminate air bubbles that keep the liquid from flowing smoothly. Crush the last 3 centimetres of the stem with a hammer and put the flowers in a saline solution (1 tablespoon of salt in 1 litre of water) for 24 hours. Next put them in a vase with 1 part glycerine and 2 parts hot water and leave them there until the solution is completely absorbed and the leaves have changed colour. The process is complete when the colour is uniform to the edges of the leaves.

Don't leave the plant in the mix too long, however, or the leaves will begin to fall. To remove excess humidity, clean the flowers carefully with a soft cotton cloth and then hang them upside down for a few days.

For best results, do this procedure in summer, when the foliage is able to absorb the solution faster.

LIST OF FLOWERS USED

Abelia
Acacia baileyana
African lily
Allium
Amaranth
Amaryllis
Anemone
Anthurium
Aralia
Artichoke
Asian bittersweet
Aster
Astilbe
Aulax cancellata
Azalea

Baby's breath
Bear grass
Beautyberry
Beech
Berzelia abrotanoides
Berzelia galpini
Black locust
Bluebell
Boat orchid
Boronia
Brassica *or* Ornamental cabbage
Brunia albiflora
Bulrush
Butterfly bush

Calathea
Calendula
Calla lily
Camellia japonica
Carnation
Celosia
Chamomile

Chocolate cosmos
Chrysanthemum
Chrysanthemum Aurinko
Chrysanthemum Bautista orange
Chrysanthemum Bouncer
Chrysanthemum Calimero pink
Chrysanthemum japanese
Chrysanthemum Jenny pink
Chrysanthemum Madiba
Chrysanthemum variegated
Clematis
Cockscomb
Cornelian cherry
Cornflower
Cosmos
Cotoneaster
Crabapple
Craspedia
Crocus
Curcuma
Cyclamen
Cymbidium

Daffodil
Dahlia
Daisy
Delphinium
Dianthus raffine
Dianthus Star Tessino
Dog rose

Eryngo
Eucalyptus
Eucalyptus globulus
Eucalyptus parvifolia
Eucalyptus pauciflora
Eucalyptus stuartiana

Fennel
Fig tree
Forget-me-not
Forsythia
Foxglove
Freesia
Fritillaria

Galax
Gaultheria
Gentian
Geranium
Gerbera
Gladiolus
Globe amaranth
Globe thistle
Gnaphalium
"Green trick" carnation
Grevillea
Guelder-rose

Hardenbergia
Hawthorn
Heather
Helichrysum
Helipterum
Hellebore
Hibiscus
Holly
Holly
Honesty
Hyacinth
Hydrangea

Iris
Ivy

Jasmine
Jatropha
Jerusalem artichoke

Kale
Kangaroo paw
Lace fern
Lady Banks rose
Lady's mantle
Laurel
Lavalle hawthorn
Lavender
Leucadendron
Leucadendron linifolium
Leucospermum cordifolium
Leucospermum cuneiforme
Lilac
Lily
Limonium
Linden
Lisianthus ·

Magnolia
Marigold
Mastic
Medlar
Milkweed
Mimosa
Mountain ash
Muhlenbergia
Muscari

Nandina
Nasturtium
Nerine
New York Aster
Nigella

Olive tree
Ozothamnus

Pampas grass
Pansy
Peony
Peruvian lily
Physalis
Pieris
Pincushion flower
Pittosporum
Pittosporum nanum
Plumbago
Poinsettia
Pomegranate
Poppy
Poppy anemone
Pothos
Primrose
Protea
Protea neriifolia
Pyracantha

Radicchio di Treviso
Ranunculus
Red chard
Red oak
Rex begonia
Rhododendron
Rose
Rosa botanica
Rose cream dream
Rosemary
Russian sage

Sage
Sagebrush
Salal
Sasanqua camellia
Shatavari

Silver ragwort
Skimmia Japonica
Smoketree
Snapdragon
Sneezeweed
Snowberry
Snowdrop
Spanish moss
St. John's wort
Stonecrop
Sunflower
Sweet pea
Sweet William

Tillandsia brachycaulos
Tillandsia caput-medusae
Tillandsia juncifolia
Tillandsia stricta
Tillandsia xerographica
Tulip

Veronica
Viburnum tinus
Virginia creeper
Vuvuzela rose

Wallflower
Waratah
Wax flower
White broom
Wild carrot
Winterberry
Wintersweet
Wisteria
Witch-hazel

Yarrow

Zinnia

BIBLIOGRAPHY

FOR MORE INFORMATION

Pietro Raitano and Cristiano Calvi, *Rose & lavoro. Dal Kenya all'Italia: l'incredibile viaggio dei fiori*, Terre di mezzo, Milan 2002

Christopher Brickell (ed.) *Royal Horticultural Society New Encyclopedia of Plants and Flowers*, Dorling Kindersley, London 1999

Keri Smith, *How to Be an Explorer of the World: Portable Life Museum*, Perigee, New York 2008

Jorn De Précy, *E il giardino creò l'uomo. Un manifesto ribelle e sentimentale per filosofi giardinieri*, Ponte alle Grazie, Milan 2012

Edith Holden, *The Country Diary of an Edwardian Lady*, Holt, Rinehart and Winston, New York 1977

Vanessa Diffenbaugh, *The Language of Flowers: A Novel*, Ballantine Books, New York 2011

Gertrude Jekyll, *The Gardener's Essential Gertrude Jekyll*, Excellent Press, Ludlow 2009

Bruno Munari, *Da cosa nasce cosa. Appunti per una metodologia concettuale*, Laterza, Bari 2010